CHRISTMAS AROUND THE WORLD COLORING BOOK

Joan O'Brien

DOVER PUBLICATIONS, INC.
Mineola, New York

PUBLISHER'S NOTE

Commemorating the birth of Jesus Christ more than 2,000 years ago, Christmas is a joyous and festive occasion celebrated in many different ways in countries around the world. Special meals, carols, Christmas trees, festive decorations, gift-giving, processions, solemn religious ceremonies, and other elements give a rich international flavor to this beloved holiday. This collection of thirty black-and-white drawings invites you to learn about a host of Yule-related customs and traditions while you enjoy coloring these illustrations that bring to vivid life the age-old story of Christmas.

Copyright

Copyright © 2003 by Joan O'Brien
All rights reserved.

Bibliographical Note

Christmas Around the World Coloring Book is a new work, first published by Dover Publications, Inc., in 2003.

DOVER *Pictorial Archive* SERIES

This book belongs to the Dover Pictorial Archive Series. You may use the designs and illustrations for graphics and crafts applications, free and without special permission, provided that you include no more than four in the same publication or project. (For permission for additional use, please write to Permissions Department, Dover Publications, Inc., 31 East 2nd Street, Mineola, N.Y. 11501.)

However, republication or reproduction of any illustration by any other graphic service, whether it be in a book or in any other design resource, is strictly prohibited.

International Standard Book Number: 0-486-42651-3

Manufactured in the United States of America
Dover Publications, Inc., 31 East 2nd Street, Mineola, N.Y. 11501

Christmas Treats

Christmas is traditionally a time for enjoying sweets and treats. This table offers a tempting array of gingerbread boys and girls, marzipan, plum pudding, candy canes, *buche de noel* (a cake shaped like a log), fruitcake, nuts—and a nutcracker—and other goodies.

Choosing a Tree

Families who live near forests often cut their own Christmas trees. It is best to select a tree before there is any snow so that the whole tree can be seen clearly. The tree is left growing in the forest until it is time to chop it down and take it home to be decorated.

City Dwellers

Those who live in the city buy their trees from vendors on the streets. The whole family can have fun choosing a tree, along with fragrant garlands and wreaths of evergreen and holly.

Australia

Christmas falls at the height of the summer season in the "Land Down Under." Instead of cold and snowy days, Australians enjoy blue skies and sunny picnics at the beach. And instead of arriving in a sleigh pulled by reindeer, Santa makes his appearance in a small, sturdy boat.

Austria

Families celebrate with Christmas trees, decorated with candies, cookies, and other ornaments, but the center of attraction is the manger scene, depicting the newborn Christ Child, with Mary and Joseph.

Belgium

In a part of Belgium called Flanders, Christmas plays are a tradition. Children portray angels, while townspeople dress in clothing similar to that worn by people of the sixteenth century as revealed in the work of the Flemish painter Pieter Bruegel.

China

Although the majority of Chinese are not Christians and do not celebrate Christmas, for those that do it is a time of joy and excitement. Children decorate their "tree of light" with paper chains, flowers, and brightly colored lanterns, while families exchange such gifts as beautiful silks, jewelry, and new clothes for the children.

Denmark

Christmas comes during the long, dark days of winter, so the warmth of home, with its fire on the hearth, candlelight, and delicious meals is very special. The people eat Christmas dinner at midnight on Christmas Eve. For dessert, they enjoy a special rice pudding. One dish has an almond in it. Whoever gets the almond can expect to enjoy good luck in the coming year.

Finland

Christmas trees are very popular in Finland because they remind people of the country's beautiful forests. Children often decorate the outdoor trees with nuts and seeds for the birds. Many Finnish country people will not eat their own Christmas dinner until the birds have eaten theirs.

France

At Christmastime a Yule log of cherry wood is carried by the family into the house, sprinkled with wine, and lit. Children leave their shoes out on Christmas Eve in hopes that *Père Noël* (Father Christmas) will fill them with presents.

France (Alsace)

In the Alsace region, a girl representing the Christ Child, or *Christkind*, wears a long, white dress and a crown of gold paper and lighted candles. In one hand she carries a plate of cookies and in the other a silver bell. She is followed by Hans Trapp, dressed in a bearskin and carrying threatening "rods." He is looking for naughty children, who are only saved by the intercession of the *Christkind*.

Germany

The Christmas tree as we know it originated in Germany. Gradually the custom developed of decorating the tree with cookies, fruit, candles, and other ornaments. In southern Germany children are locked out of the room where the tree stands until they hear a little bell ringing. This tells them the Christ Child has come and is now leaving through the open window. Children are often told that the Christ Child brought the tree as well as the gifts.

Germany

Preparations for Christmas start with Advent, which means "the coming of Christ." An Advent wreath is lighted with four candles, one for each Sunday in December. On St. Nicholas Day (December 6), children fill their shoes with hay, straw, or carrots for St. Nicholas' horse or donkey. Also, children write letters to the Christ Child. They hang them in the window and sprinkle sugar on them to catch the Christ Child's eye when he passes by. When they awake in the morning, if they have been good, their shoes are filled with toys and goodies.

Great Britain

Groups of children visit their neighbors at Christmas and serenade them with traditional Christmas carols.

Often, the neighbors offer carolers special treats and something warm to drink.

Great Britain

A traditional Christmas dinner means roast goose, mince pie, and plum pudding decorated with holly and ablaze with flaming brandy. Beside each person's place is a cracker—a brightly colored paper tube filled with trinkets. When snapped open, the cracker makes a pop or cracking sound.

Great Britain

"Boxing Day" is celebrated on December 26—the day after Christmas. It began as a day when gifts were "boxed up" and offered to the poor, and it is still customary to give money to employees and tradesmen who have performed services throughout the year, and to exchange gifts with family and friends.

Great Britain

Kissing under the mistletoe is an old English custom that may have originated in early folk festivals. One story says the custom began with ancient Britons who hung a sprig of mistletoe above their doors to scare away witches. A kiss was quickly given to anyone who passed through the doorway. It's still a good excuse to steal a kiss!

Greece

St. Nicholas is the patron saint of Greek sailors, among whom fishing is a major occupation. On Christmas Eve children go from house to house singing carols to the accompaniment of drums and the tinkling of triangles. Boys often carry model boats decorated with gold-painted nuts. Householders give the children dried figs, almonds, walnuts and sweets, or even small gifts. At home, where Christmas bread is served, good luck comes to the one who finds a coin in a slice of bread.

Iraq

On Christmas Eve Christian children read about the birth of Jesus. Then the family makes a fire of thorn branches. When the flames have died down, each family member jumps over the ashes three times and makes a wish.

Italy

During Christmas a *presepio* or manger, is a common feature in homes and public places. The tradition was begun by St. Francis of Assisi, and continues today when children and their families gather around a manger symbolizing where Jesus was born. There, Mary and Joseph and the infant were warmed by the breath of an ox and a donkey, so these animals are always included in the stable.

Mexico

A favorite Christmas tradition is breaking the *piñata*. It is an earthenware jar suspended from the ceiling and filled with fruits, nuts, and candy. One by one, the children are blindfolded and given a chance to break the *piñata* with a stick. When someone succeeds, there is a scramble for the goodies that have fallen to the floor.

The Netherlands

On December fifth, St. Nicholas or *Sinterklaas* arrives by boat in the city of Amsterdam, of which he is patron saint. He then mounts a white horse to be greeted by the mayor. Children follow him through the town. Nearly every city and village has its own *Sinterklaas* parade. At home, children fill wooden shoes with hay and carrots for St. Nicholas' horse.

24

Norway

After a big dinner on Christmas Eve families hide all the brooms in the house. A long time ago people thought that witches and evil spirits came out that night and they didn't want the witches riding their brooms. Norwegians also put wheat on trees or poles shaped like tree branches. If many sparrows eat the wheat, it means a good growing year for crops.

Poland

A huge feast is held on Christmas Eve. To honor the Star of Bethlehem, however, the meal does not begin until the first star of night appears. Santa is "Gwiazdor" ("star man")—for the North Star. He visits children on Christmas Eve, bringing presents. Candles shine in the window to welcome the Christ Child.

Puerto Rico

On January twelfth a colorful celebration known as "Bethlehem Day" takes place, featuring a parade of children marching through the streets. They are led by three other children dressed as Wise Men, with gifts for the infant Jesus in their hands.

Russia

On Christmas Eve it is customary for a priest to visit the house, accompanied by altar boys carrying holy water. Making his way through the house, the priest sprinkles a little holy water in each room.

Spain

Families go to church on Christmas morning, and again on January sixth, twelve days after Christmas. On the night of the sixth, children put their shoes, filled with barley for the Wise Men's camels, on the balcony or doorstep. In the morning, they hope to find the barley gone and the shoes filled with toys and fruit.

Sweden

Celebration of the holiday season begins on St. Lucia Day, December 13. Lucia lived in the fourth century and is believed to have used candles placed in a wreath on her head to light her way while bringing food to prisoners. Today, a young girl is chosen in each family to awake early in the morning and serve breakfast to her family. Dressed in a white robe, with a red sash and a crown of candles on her head, she serves a traditional meal of buns flavored with saffron.

United States

The custom of hanging stockings from the mantelpiece comes from England. The story is that while coming down the chimney, Santa Claus dropped some gold coins, which fell into a stocking hanging there to dry. Since then, children hang their stockings on the mantel in the hopes that Santa Claus will fill them with gifts. They also leave milk and cookies to refresh Santa as he makes his rounds on Christmas Eve.

The Nutcracker Ballet

The Nutcracker, a ballet danced to the music of Tchaikovsky, is a traditional Christmas favorite. It tells the story of little Clara, whose nutcracker doll is transformed into a handsome prince. They travel through windswept snow to the Kingdom of Sweets.